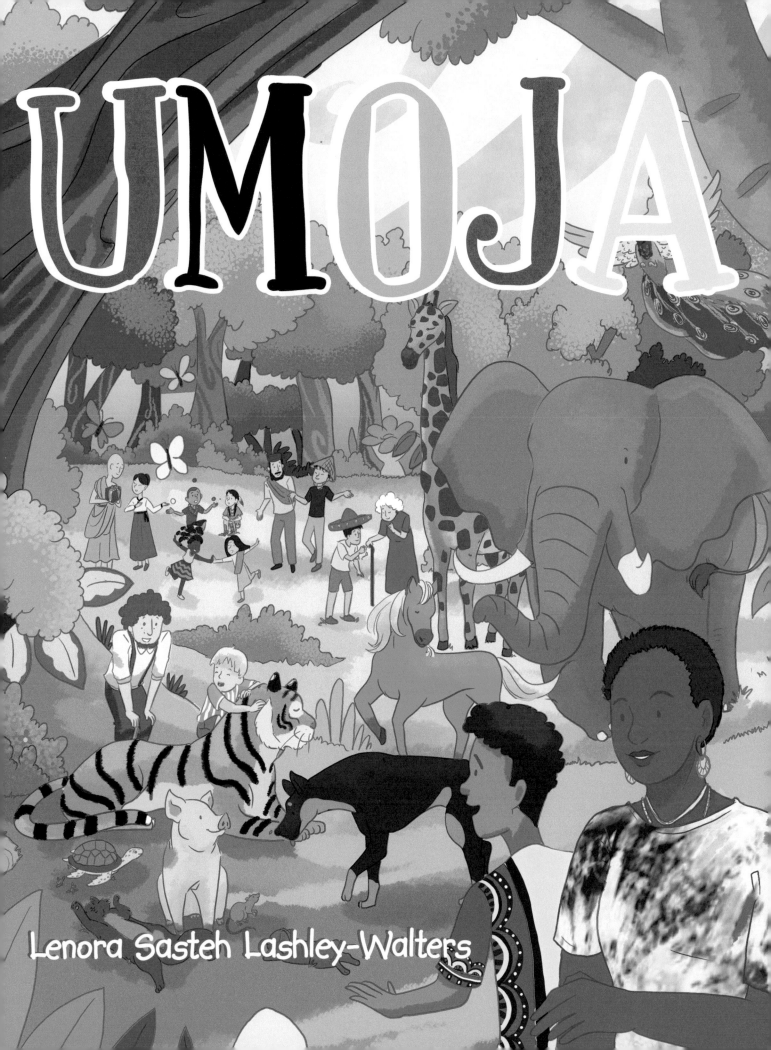

UMOJA

Lenora Sasteh Lashley-Walters

Balboa Press books may be ordered through booksellers or by contacting:

Balboa Press
A Division of Hay House
1663 Liberty Drive
Bloomington, IN 47403
www.balboapress.com
844-682-1282

Because of the dynamic nature of the Internet, any web addresses or links contained in this book may have changed since publication and may no longer be valid. The views expressed in this work are solely those of the author and do not necessarily reflect the views of the publisher, and the publisher hereby disclaims any responsibility for them.

Any people depicted in stock imagery provided by Getty Images are models, and such images are being used for illustrative purposes only.
Certain stock imagery © Getty Images.

ISBN: 978-1-9822-6251-8 (sc)
ISBN: 978-1-9822-6252-5 (e)

Library of Congress Control Number: 2021901110

Print information available on the last page.

Balboa Press rev. date: 01/29/2021

UMOJA

This book is dedicated to my five children and my grandchildren. And to all of the children I have ever taught. Readers are leaders!

In the beginning was I.

I willed to be no-thing,

still and realized.

Let there be light.

I became sound.
And I said, "Let
there be light."

I became the sun,
who smiled on the
Earth that is I.

I became day,

and night.

I became air.

I became the water.

I became trees
and flowers.

I became all creatures,
from the little ant,
to the big elephant.

I became sounds. I became thoughts. I became pictures, too.

I became YOU,
and your Mommy
and Daddy too!

There's a connection between she and he; you and me; they and we. We're all connected in unity. It's Umoja that binds us together you see.

UMOJA means unity.
The unity in all you see.
Umoja means unity
that binds you to me.

THE END

Printed in the United States
By Bookmasters